First published in Great Britain in 1993 by Andersen Press Ltd., 20 Vauxhall
Bridge Road, London SW1 2SA. Published in Australia by Random House
Australia Pty., 20 Alfred Street, Milsons Point, Sydney, NSW 2061. All rights
reserved. Colour separated in Switzerland by Photolitho AG,
Offsetreproduktionen, Gossau, Zurich. Printed and bound in Italy by Grafiche
AZ, Verona.

10 9 8 7 6 5 4 3 2 1

British Library Cataloguing in Publication Data available.

ISBN 0 86264 361 9

This book has been printed on acid-free paper

A CREEPY CRAWLY SONG BOOK

LYRICS BY
HIAWYN ORAM
MUSIC BY
CARL DAVIS
PICTURES BY
SATOSHI KITAMURA

ANDERSEN PRESS
LONDON

CONTENTS

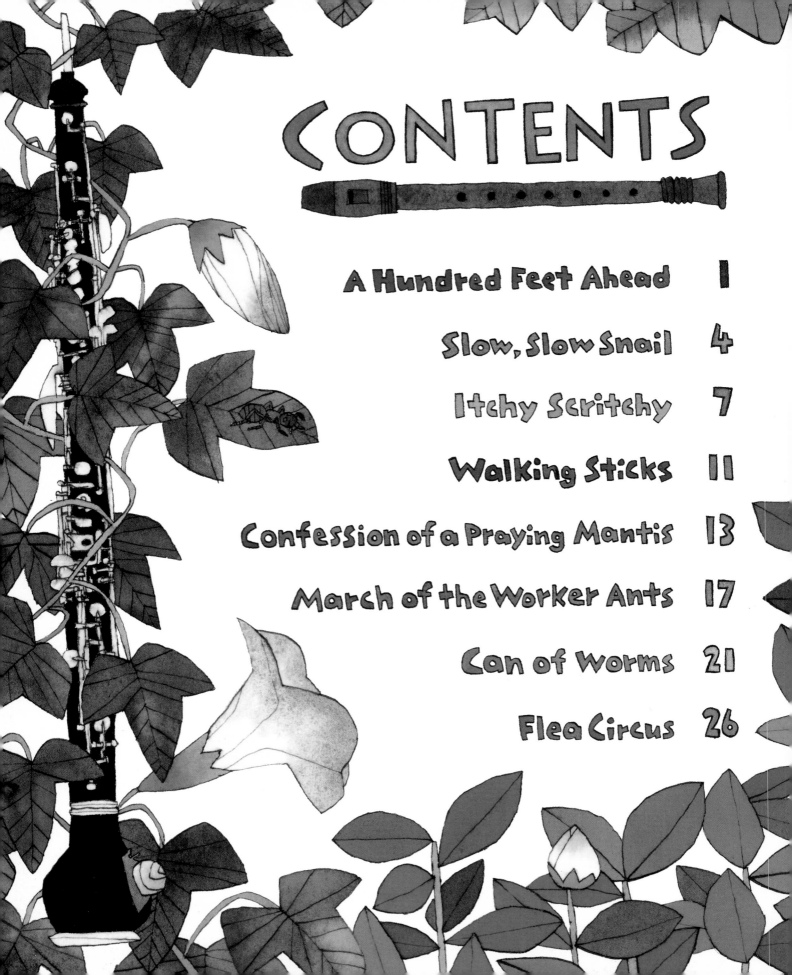

A Hundred Feet Ahead

Tempo di Gavotte: Moderato   2nd time, a tempo

mf (stiffly)   *sim.*   1. I've a | cent-i – ped-al bod-y, I've a

hun-dred feet in all, I can | move a – bout like light-ning, I don't

have to creep or crawl. I can | dash a – bout the green house, I can

dart with-out a thought, I'm so | quick to seize my quar-ry It don't

know that it's been caught.

A HUNDRED FEET AHEAD
(Dance of the Centipede)

I've a centipedal body,
I've a hundred feet in all,
I can move about like lightning,
I don't have to creep or crawl.
I can dash about the greenhouse,
I can dart without a thought,
I'm so quick to seize my quarry
It don't know that it's been caught.

And when it comes to footwork,
With the kind of legs I've got,
You should really see my cancan
And my rumba and gavotte.

For... I've... this... centipedal body,
It's the way that I've been bred,
And no matter what I'm doing
I'm a hundred feet ahead.
I can rush around the garden,
I can burrow through the ground,
I can get away from danger
Fast as danger comes around.

And when it comes to footwork,
With the kind of legs I've got,
You should really see my Charleston
And my centipedal trot.

Slow, Slow Snail

Very slow

1. Slow, slow snail, Slow, slow snail, Tak- ing for-ev - er to

cross a leaf, If you don't hur-ry up you will come to grief, Slow, slow snail.

2. Slow, slow snail, Slow, slow snail, What- e- ver you do, don't cross that path: There's a

plump young thrush in the stone birdbath With a bead-y eye on your shin - ing trail,

5

Slow, slow snail.____ 3. Slow, slow snail,_ Slow, slow snail, You took for-ev-er to

cross that leaf. You could-n't make haste and you came to grief In the beak of a com-mon or

gar-den thief. Now all that's left is your shin-ing trail,____ But no slow snail,

no slow snail, no slow snail.____

SLOW, SLOW SNAIL

Slow, slow snail,
Slow, slow snail,
Taking forever to cross a leaf,
If you don't hurry up you will come to grief,
Slow, slow snail.

Slow, slow snail,
Slow, slow snail,
Whatever you do, don't cross that path:
There's a plump young thrush in the stone birdbath
With a beady eye on your shining trail,
Slow, slow snail.

Slow, slow snail,
Slow, slow snail,
You took forever to cross that leaf.
You couldn't make haste and you came to grief
In the beak of a common or garden thief.
Now all that's left is your shining trail,
But no slow snail,
No slow snail,
No... slow... snail...

Itchy Scritchy

Allegretto

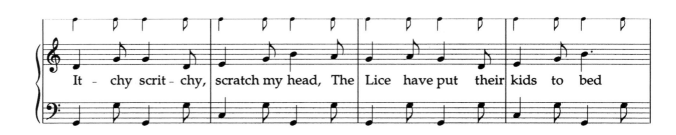

It - chy scrit - chy, scratch my head, The Lice have put their kids to bed

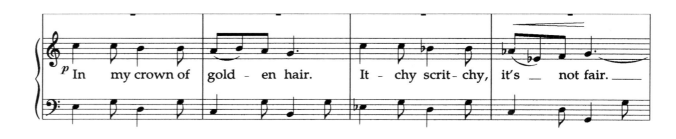

In my crown of gold - en hair. It - chy scrit - chy, it's __ not fair. ___

Su - sie's hair is nic - er,

Em - ma's hair is long - er, Jas - on's hair is thick - er,

cresc. *poco* *a* *poco*

And - y's hair is stron - ger, Mar - y's hair is dirt - y,

f

Dan's sits up and begs,_____ *f* So why's it on - ly MY hair

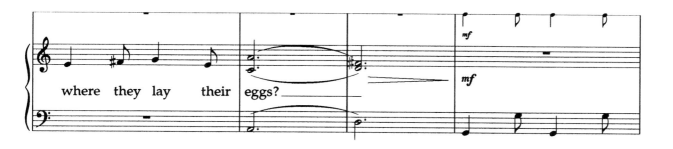

mf

where they lay their eggs?_____ *mf*

It - chy scrit - chy, scratch my head, The Lice have put their

kids to bed. It - chy scrit - chy, scratch and shout: How'll I EV - ER

get them out!

sim.

mf

pp

ITCHY SCRITCHY

Itchy scritchy, scratch my head,
The Lice have put their kids to bed
In my crown of golden hair.
Itchy scritchy, it's not fair.

Susie's hair is nicer,
Emma's hair is longer,
Jason's hair is thicker,
Andy's hair is stronger,
Mary's hair is dirty,
Dan's sits up and begs,
So why's it always MY hair
Where they lay their eggs?

Itchy scritchy, scratch my head,
The Lice have put their kids to bed.
Itchy scritchy, scratch and shout:
How'll I EVER get them out!

Walking Sticks

Andante ♩. = 60   First Voices

Still as the night

When the wind drops, Still as a kite When the breeze stops,

Second Voices

Still as the grave, Sil – ent and cold, Still as a tale That's

All

nev – er been told, Till the sun sets And the night falls.

Confession of a Praying Mantis

Andante

1. Oh, they think I'm ver-y pi-ous And they think I'm ver-y good, 'Cos it looks as though I'm pray-ing Like a ho-ly Brah-man would; And it

looks as though I'm pat – ient, Oth – er world – ly, on my knees, Beg – ging

fav – ours of our Mak – er, Say – ing thank you, say – ing please. ____

poco più mosso

2. But the truth is I'm not pray – ing, I'm not

rev' – rent, I'm no saint, That is on – ly the im – pres – sion And the

pic - ture that I paint; No, the truth is I'm not god - ly, I'm un -

- grate-ful, and I'm rude, And the on - ly words of prayer I know Are

Tempo 1

GIM - ME, GIM - ME FOOD.

CONFESSION OF A PRAYING MANTIS

Oh, they think I'm very pious
And they think I'm very good,
'Cos it looks as though I'm praying
Like a holy Brahman would;
And it looks as though I'm patient,
Otherworldly, on my knees,
Begging favours of our Maker,
Saying thank you, saying please.

But the truth is I'm not praying,
I'm not rev'rent, I'm no saint,
That is only the impression
And the picture that I paint;
No, the truth is I'm not godly,
I'm ungrateful, and I'm rude,
And the only words of prayer I know
Are GIMME, GIMME FOOD.

March of the Worker Ants

Moderato

Left, right, left; left, right, left. 1. The

Sol – dier Ants are here to say We'll

guard the nest as best we may, For the

Queen is lay – ing her eggs to – day. Left, right,

left; left, right, left. 2. The

Nurse-maid Ants are stand-ing by To wash and feed the young lar -

- vae; The Clean - er Ants have cleared the ground Of

scraps and husks left ly - ing round, For the Queen is lay-ing her eggs to -

Repeat for verses 3 & 4

- day. Left, right, left; left, right, left. 3., 4. & 5. The

much faster

(5.) Sol- dier Ants will guard the nest, The Nurse-maid Ants will do their best, The

MARCH OF THE WORKER ANTS

Left, right, left; left, right, left.
The Soldier Ants are here to say
We'll guard the nest as best we may,
For the Queen is laying her eggs today.
Left, right, left; left, right, left.

The Nursemaid Ants are standing by
To wash and feed the young larvae;
The Cleaner Ants have cleared the ground
Of scraps and husks left lying round,
For the Queen is laying her eggs today.
Left, right, left; left, right, left.

The Miller Ants have ground the wheat
Until it's fine enough to eat;
The Farmer Ants have milked the herd
Of fat young aphids: pass the word,
For the Queen is laying her eggs today.
Left, right, left; left, right, left.

The Barrel Ants are filled to burst
With honeydew in case of thirst;
The Gardener Ants have grown a crop
Of fine fresh fungus and can't stop,
For the Queen is laying her eggs today.
Left, right, left; left, right, left.

(Much faster)
The Soldier Ants will guard the nest,
The Nursemaid Ants will do their best,
The Cleaner Ants have cleared the ground,
The Miller Ants the wheat have ground,
The Farmer Ants have milked the herd,
The Barrel Ants are full, my word,
The Gardener Ants have grown a feast,
While the Hunter Ants have bagged a beast,
For the Queen has LAID her eggs today.
Hurray, hurray, hurray! Hurray, hurray, hurray!...

Can of Worms

Moderato

1. A can of wrig - gling,

wig - gling worms Stood by a bab - bling brook; The

talk was all of who'd be next Up - on the fish - er - man's

hook.   "Not me," said the Pink,   "I'm far   too thin."   "Not

me," said the Grey,   "I   won't   give in."   "Not me,"   said the Brown.   "It's

not   my line."   "Then you," said the fish-er-man, "you'll   do fine".___

2nd time molto rall.

Repeat for verse 2 Andante

quieter

3. An emp – ty can with-
-out a worm Stood by that bab – bling brook; The
talk was none, they all had gone To bait the fish- er -man's

hook. "I jumped," said the Pink, "in - to a trout." "I

wound," said the Grey, "now let me out." "I swam," said the Brown, "but

far too late." "That's right," said the fish - er - man,

accel.

"you did great!"_____

CAN OF WORMS

A can of wriggling, wiggling worms
Stood by a babbling brook;
The talk was all of who'd be next
Upon the fisherman's hook.
"Not me," said the Pink, "I'm far too thin."
"Not me," said the Grey, "I won't give in."
"Not me," said the Brown, "it's not my line."
"Then you," said the fisherman, "you'll do fine."

A can of wriggling, wiggling worms
Stood by that babbling brook;
The talk was all of how to get
From off a fisherman's hook.
"You jump," said the Pink, "you can't go wrong."
"You wind," said the Grey, "but don't take long."
"You swim," said the Brown, "or else you float."
"That's right," said the fisherman, "down a throat."

An empty can without a worm
Stood by that babbling brook;
The talk was none, they all had gone
To bait the fisherman's hook.
"I jumped," said the Pink, "into a trout."
"I wound," said the Grey, "now let me out."
"I swam," said the Brown, "but far too late."
"That's right," said the fisherman, "you did great!"

Flea Circus

Tempo 1

3. Cat fleas, Fat fleas, Ham - ster and Mouse, And

ev - ry kind of flea from hedge - row and house,

Come and take your seat, get your full mom-ent's worth At the

Great flea Cir-cus that's the Smal- lest Show on Earth!

f

col. Bass Drum

R.H.

p

Battle of the Stags

Allegro ma non troppo   *menacing*

with tambourine
p

1. There was no growl, there was no snarl, There was no warn- ing sound,_____ As Beet- le One, that Might- y Stag, Pre- pared to stand his ground._____ For Beet- le Two, so young and keen, Would make the branch his

BATTLE OF THE STAGS

(With drums and background percussion)

There was no growl, there was no snarl,
There was no warning sound,
As Beetle One, that Mighty Stag,
Prepared to stand his ground.
For Beetle Two, so young and keen,
Would make the branch his own
And raised his horns to give the sign
He'd fight this out alone.

The Mighty Stag, the young Greenhorn
Now locked in deadly wrest,
And who could see the other off
Would be the final test.
So up and down that slender branch
Those battling beetles went.
Their armour held and gave no sign
Of chip or chink or dent.

And then at last the Mighty Stag
A winning grasp had found;
And, lifting up the young Greenhorn,
He threw him to the ground.
The Greenhorn lay defeated there
But still one punch would pack;
And raised his head and loudly hissed,
"O.K. - BUT I'LL BE BACK!"

Busy Bee

Brightly, Allegro

1. The busi-ness-man is busy, he is busy be-ing busy; The doc-tor is so bus-y that she some-times drops; The por-ter on the plat-form, he is ver-y, ver-y bus-y; The moth-er of four child-ren nev-er

stops. But of all the ver-y bus-y things that you or I will see The

rit. bus-i-est of all of them must be the bus-y bee.

a tempo Bus-y in the bush-es and

bus-y in the field, Sip-ping all the nec-tar that each

BUSY BEE

The businessman is busy, he is busy being busy;
The doctor is so busy that she sometimes drops;
The porter on the platform, he is very, very busy;
The mother of four children never stops.
But of all the very busy things that you or I will see
The busiest of all of them must be the busy bee.

Busy in the bushes and busy in the field,
Sipping all the nectar that each flower can yield,
Busy in the beehive and busy in the trees,
Busy feeding future busy, busy, busy bees.

The hornet is so busy, it just buzzes it's so busy;
The firefly is a-busy giving off a glow;
The butterfly is flat out going flitter flutter flat out;
The slug is kept quite busy going slow.
But of all the very busy things that you or I will see
The busiest of all of them must be the busy bee.

Busy in the bushes and busy in the field,
Sipping all the nectar that each flower can yield,
Busy in the beehive and busy in the trees,
Busy feeding future busy, busy, busy bees.

The businessman is busy, he is busy being busy;
The housewife is so busy that she sometimes weeps;
The waitress in the diner, she is very, very busy;
The watchman who's on duty never sleeps.
But of all the very busy things that you or I will see
The busiest of all of them must be the busy bee.
Busy, busy, busy, busy, busy, busy, busy...

Living a Day

LIVING A DAY
(Song of the Mayflies)

Born in the morning,
Married at noon,
Buried at sunset:
Death, you're too soon.
Living a lifetime
All in a day,
Living a lifetime
For one day in May.

Born for the moment,
Caught in the dance:
Come, let us take it
While there's a chance.
Living a lifetime
All in a day,
Living a lifetime
For one day in May.

Born to be mayflies,
Born not to last,
Seizing the present
As it flies past.
Living a lifetime
All in a day,
Living a lifetime
For one day in May.

The Black Widow's Waltz

THE BLACK WIDOW'S WALTZ

Black Widow's grieving:
Her husbands keep leaving
Her children and her on their own.
She's fiercely berating
Such cowardly mating
That leaves a poor widow alone.

Black Widow's wailing,
And Black Widow's railing,
And Black Widow's dead against men.
She's pursing and pouting
And def'nitely doubting
She'll ever get married again.

Black Widow's crying:
Her husbands keep dying
As soon as each wedding is done.
She's loudly complaining
There're no men remaining,
Forgetting she ATE EVERY ONE!

A Creepy Crawly Caterpillar

Slowly

1. A creep-y crawl-y cat-er-pil-lar

Lay up-on a leaf,_____ His bod-y full of milk-weed sap, His

thoughts weighed down with grief.___ "I do not have a fea-thered plume, Nor

yet a vel-vet wing;___ I can-not flit, I can-not fly, I

am an ug - ly thing.___ And yet I'm sure that deep in - side, A-

-struggling to be free,___ There is some oth - er char - act- er, There

1. and 2.

is an - o - ther me."___

2. Then
3. And

3. rit.

but - ter- fly - that's me!"___

A CREEPY CRAWLY CATERPILLAR

A creepy crawly caterpillar
Lay upon a leaf,
His body full of milkweed sap,
His thoughts weighed down with grief.
"I do not have a feathered plume,
Nor yet a velvet wing;
I cannot flit, I cannot fly,
I am an ugly thing.
And yet I'm sure that deep inside,
A-struggling to be free,
There is some other character,
There is another me."

Then creepy crawly caterpillar
Made himself a bed
And tucked up tight and fell asleep
And dreamed his dreams instead.
"I do so want a feathered plume
And, more, a velvet wing;
I long to flit, I long to fly,
To be a lovely thing.
I am so sure that deep inside,
A-struggling to be free,
There is some other character,
There is another me."

And as it was, that caterpillar
From his sleep did wake,
And took a breath and stretched a leg
And gave himself a shake.
"I seem to have a feathered plume
A velvet painted wing;
I seem to flit, I seem to fly,
I am a lovely thing.
I was so sure deep down inside,
A-struggling to be free,
There was some other character:
A butterfly - that's me!"

Uurgh, Eeegh, Ugh

Slowly

sempre p

1. Uurgh, eegh, ugh, A green and slim – y slug,
   (1.) Have you
   (2.) Who could

2. ev – er met such a wob – bi – ly blob, Such a slip – per – y, slith – er – y, slug-gard – ly slob, But an –
   ev – er love such a wob – bi – ly blob, Such a liv – er – y, sliv – er – y slug-gard – ly slob, But an –

3. – oth – er slug? An – oth – er slug!

Mama Mosquito's Midnight Whine

"A lit-tle bit-ty meal,___ A lit-tle drink of blood,___ Is

all I ask of you, Bab-y, sweet rose-bud.___ A

lit-tle frag-rant nip:___ Can that be such a sin?___ Now

o-pen up your net, Bab-y, please let me in."___ mm ___

MAMA MOSQUITO'S MIDNIGHT WHINE

The midnight hour is creepin',
Baby lies a-sleepin'
Underneath her veil of net so fine;
She stirs and wakes to hear it
And she doesn't know to fear it,
Mama Mosquito's Midnight Whine.

(With whining effects)

"A little bitty meal,
A little drink of blood,
Is all I ask of you,
Baby, sweet rosebud.
A little fragrant nip:
Can that be such a sin?
Now open up your net,
Baby, please let me in."

The midnight dew is glist'nin',
Baby is a-list'nin'
Underneath her veil of net so fine;
She smiles where she is layin'
At the band she thinks is playin'
Mama Mosquito's Midnight Whine.

"A little bitty meal,
A little drink of blood,
Is all I ask of you,
Baby, sweet rosebud.
A little bitty sip:
Can that do any harm?
My laying time is near.
Baby, throw out an arm."

The gate of dawn unlatches,
Baby frets and scratches
Underneath her veil of net so fine;
She cries where she is layin',
Bitten hard by all that playin'
Of Mama Mosquito's Midnight Whine ...
Mama Mosquito's ... Midnight ... Whine (fading) ...

Lament of the House Fly

Andantino

2nd and 3rd times

ZZZ _____ ZZZ _____

2. & 3. I'd

1. Oh, to be a Rob – ber Fly, some oth – er fly but

me, _____ A Crane Fly or a Fruit Fly or a

3rd time go to ⊕

Broth – er Fly, not me; _____ The House Fly is so

hat – ed, It's so hound – ed, un – der – rat – ed, That I'd

Repeat for verses 2 & 3

rath – er be most an – y fly but me.

House Fly's fate's al – lot – ted – There you see:

All clap

f

pp

I've just been swat – ted, And a Dead Fly, ver – y

pp

51

Dead Fly, NOW THAT'S ME. _____

Repeat ad lib.

zzzz _____ zzzz _____

p *pp*

LAMENT OF THE HOUSE FLY

Oh, to be a Robber Fly, some other fly but me,
A Crane Fly or a Fruit Fly or a Brother Fly, not me;
The House Fly is so hated,
It's so hounded, underrated,
That I'd rather be most any fly but me.

I'd rather be a Caddis Fly, a Dung Fly, or a Drone,
I'd even be a Tsetse, working jungles on my own.
The House Fly's life is fated,
From the start incriminated.
Oh, I'd rather be most any fly but me.

I'd rather be a Flower Fly, a Stalk-Eye, or a Bee;
I'd love to be a Horse Fly in a hunting stablery.
The House Fly's fate's allotted -
There you see: I've just been swatted,
And a Dead Fly, very Dead Fly, NOW THAT'S ME.

Ladybird's Lullaby

Very Slow

p · *sim.*

1. Hush, lit-tle love-bugs, don't say a word; The

moon's in the sky and the night-jar is heard; The glow-worms are glow-ing, the

Repeat for verses 2. & 3.

fire-flies peep, And you, my lit-tle love-bugs, must now go to sleep.

LADYBIRD'S LULLABY

Hush, little lovebugs, don't say a word;
The moon's in the sky and the nightjar is heard;
The glowworms are glowing, the fireflies peep,
And you, my little lovebugs, must now go to sleep.

Hush, little darlings, don't make a sound;
The stars are a-lit and the dew's on the ground;
The bat wings are whirring, the owl is awake,
And you should be in bed, yes, *now for heaven's sake!*

Hush, little lovebugs, don't say a word;
The moon's in the sky and the nightjar is heard;
The glowworms are glowing, the fireflies peep,
And you, my little lovebugs, are now ... fast ... aslee ... eep ...